THE POWER OF THOUGHT CHILDREN'S BOOK SERIES

IS WHAT I'M THINKING TRUE?

Written by Amber Raymond & Lynn McLaughlin

Illustrated by Allysa Batin

Copyright © 2022 by Amber Raymond and Lynn McLaughlin,
in Canada

All rights reserved. No part of this book may be reproduced in any form or by an electronic or mechanical means, including information storage and retrieval systems, without written permission in writing from the copyright owners except by a reviewer who may quote brief passages in a review.

Illustrated by Allysa Batin

ISBN: 978-1-7750017-8-2 (paperback)
ISBN: 978-1-7750017-9-9 (ebook)

Printed by Print Works
382 Devonshire Road
Windsor, Ontario N8Y 2L4

https://lynnmclaughlin.com
https://www.messsmakers.com

We all feel many emotions. The characters on the planet Tezra glow in the following colours to match how they are feeling.

<u>Red</u>	<u>Orange</u>	<u>Blue</u>	<u>Yellow</u>	<u>Green</u>	<u>Purple</u>
Anger	Scared	Sad	Surprised	Happy	Lonely
Frustration	Worried	Disappoint-ed	Unexpected Event	1 Believe in Myself	
	Uncertain				

Are You Up For A Challenge?

- Can you see when each character's feelings are changing?
- Can you tell by the look on their faces, by body language or the words they are using? Maybe you can tell by the colour of their glow.
- Have you ever felt the same way? How do you express your own feelings?

"Today you will each get to show us how much you've learned." Opal announced **happily**.

"Hey Epido, you were orange and then you turned green. How did you do that?" Lazu asked.

"Wow, look at all of you feeling **confident** and ready to take the test," said Opal. "Let's do it!" They shouted.

"When we have strong emotions it's hard to think clearly and see the truth and what is real.

Sometimes our **worries** can keep us from trying new things and succeeding."

Thankfully,
You Can Check the Facts Too!

1. Ask yourself what you are worried about.
2. Think about other times when you were worried but did well in the end.
3. Ask yourself what you did to succeed.
4. Focus on the truth.

Vocabulary

Worried - A feeling of being nervous about something you think is going to happen

Happy – A feeling that makes you smile

Positive – Thinking thoughts that make you feel good

Confident - Feeling sure of yourself and your abilities

Succeed - Accomplishing something you worked hard on or hoped for

Fact - Something that is known to have happened or to exist

Like You, Every Crystal is Unique!

Did you notice the characters are all named after crystals?

Some crystals look like simple rocks, and others look like they're from another planet. No matter their appearance, they all make you feel a sense of wonder when you see the way they shine.

Also known as rocks, gemstones, and minerals, crystals are formed through geological processes by heat and pressure underground. Working with crystals can help you transform into the most powerful version of yourself by guiding you to see how incredible you truly are.

Carnelian (*Carnuli*): empowerment, focus, action and confidence

Opal (*Opal*): creativity, renewed hope, good karma, balance, self-regulation

Lapis Lazuli (*Lazu*): intuition, education, communication and problem solving

Sardonyx (*Nyx*): empowerment, confidence, leadership, courage, growth and boundaries

Epidote (Epido): energize, healthy, **strengthen**, provide hope, open you to love and joy

Amber Raymond
BA, BSW, MSW, RSW

WWW.MESSSMAKERS.COM

As a Social Worker, Amber is an advocate for unconventional, evidence-based coping strategies and is devoted to her friends and family.
She is passionate about child mental health, lifelong self-care practices, self-exploration, self-love, and holistic wellbeing.

When not practicing social work, Amber likes to research new, effective methods to overcoming life's mental and emotional challenges.